G000088151

JUDAISM

Clive A. Lawton
Headmaster: King David High School, Liverpool

Clive Erricker
Lecturer in Arts Education: The University of Warwick

SERIES EDITOR: CLIVE ERRICKER

Lecturer in Arts Education
University of Warwick

About the Themes in Religion series

This series of books offers a lively and accessible introduction to the six main world religions for students taking GCSE Religious Studies. The books can be used separately to study one religious tradition, or they can be used together, to investigate one theme across the traditions, such as beliefs, worship, pilgrimage or values. The section on values shows how each religion reacts to everyday life and the modern world. The spreads offer class activities and assignments that relate to coursework requirements and encourage further research, and each book provides a glossary of important terms and a reading list.

Each spread is self-contained and presents an important aspect of each religion. Through carefully chosen photographs, clear text and relevant quotations from scriptures and believers, students will learn about each religion and the living impact it has for believers today. The wide variety of assignments help pupils to evaluate what they have read, suggest activities to further their understanding, and raise issues for them to reflect on.

We hope that these books will provide students of all abilities with a stimulating introduction to these religions, and that the enjoyment of using them matches that of producing them.

Clive Erricker

Thank You
We would like to thank Alan Brine, Jane Erricker, Sara Leviten and Lilian Weatherley for their revisions, suggestions and unstinting support.

About Judaism

There are only about twelve million Jews in the whole world. As a general rule, they are Jews because their mothers were Jews. Thus they are members of a huge clan or tribe that has been scattered over the world for two thousand years, played a significant part in the various countries in which they have found themselves, but at the same time kept a sense that they inherit a tradition which finds its roots in the earliest history of the Jewish people.

There are many Jews, fiercely proud of being Jewish, who do not follow many or, indeed, any Jewish practices. Others might keep some of the festivals or traditions for reasons other than a belief in God's commands. Being Jewish is a cultural as much as a religious identity.

It is perhaps worth noting what is not in this book. Firstly, there is no section on pilgrimages. There are no genuine pilgrimage places for Jews nowadays and they are as likely to go to Russia to support Soviet Jews, to Auschwitz to mourn their dead or to the East End of London to find their roots as they are to go anywhere 'religious'. Secondly, there is no section on 'founders' or exemplars. In general Jews do not have a cult of personalities.

This book attempts to look beneath the surface at some of the driving forces for Jews and Judaism and to explore Judaism as a contemporary religion with things to say (and struggles to contend with) in the here and now. There is not much accessible material that reveals how Jews might think – only what they might do – and it is that need that has directed the choice of material in this book.

Clive A. Lawton
Clive Erricker

CONTENTS

BELIEFS

THE PRESENCE OF GOD

What makes somewhere special?

● Is there a place that reminds you of someone special and precious to you? Describe this place to a partner and say who it reminds you of and why.

Below is a comment made by Judy, a young woman from London, about being at the Western Wall:

'I felt like I was at home everywhere in Israel but the Western Wall was something quite special. When I got up close and touched the stones I just burst into tears. I don't know why. I'm not even religious. In a way I felt I was privileged to be able to be there when so many other Jews wanted to be.'

The Shekhina

Jews believe that God has a personality and that the sense of God's presence can be experienced in particular places. This Godly presence is known in Hebrew as the **Shekhina,** and it is at these special places that they often feel particularly close to God.

A young Jew praying
at the Western Wall
of the Temple in Jerusalem

Jews also believe that God promised them the land of Israel, and for this reason they feel related to and responsible for it in a religious and not just a patriotic way, even if the land itself is not always fertile or welcoming.

Here a Russian Jew who emigrated to Israel in 1908 talks about his home in the Negev desert and explains this feeling:

'When we founded Sde Boker there was nothing there at all except rocks and sand. We felt a bit like the Israelites in the Wilderness, but we weren't travelling, we had arrived. A few romantics were moved by the power of the desert but I was more moved by the power of the Jews to make the land blossom again as the prophets had foretold.'

ASSIGNMENTS

● Imagine you are a guide at the Western Wall in Jerusalem. Write an explanation to the scene in the picture in order to help the people who are with you understand what is happening and why.

● Make a list of up to four places where you think Jews might believe the Shekhina is particularly to be found. Use the books on page 64 or others to help you. Write a brief explanation about each one of these places, saying why they are important places for Jews.

KEY WORDS

Shekhina

WHAT IS TORAH?

Listening to God

A narrow way of describing the **Torah** is to say it is the first five books of the Bible: Genesis, Exodus, Leviticus, Numbers and Deuteronomy. Sometimes 'Torah' is translated as 'the Law', but this is inadequate, as this rabbi explains:

'It makes me so cross when people talk about "the Law" instead of using the Hebrew word "Torah". After all, it includes history, theology, guidance, morals, ethics, legends, songs, and that's just the written Torah. If you include the Oral Torah you've got 3,000 years of teaching, commentary and stories. Calling Torah the Law is like calling – I don't know – there isn't anything you can compare the Torah to!'

Some Jews believe that God also gave to Moses on Mount Sinai an oral Torah which explained the written Torah. Eventually these teachings were written down and commented on in the Talmud and other texts (see page 38). The whole body of traditional teaching and interpretation is also called 'Torah'. To study Torah is to study the Jewish religion.

One of the most important statements in the Torah is called the Shema. 'Shema' means 'listen'. The first sentence is 'Listen Israel, the Lord is our God, the Lord is One.' This helps to explain that the Torah is God's guidance to Israel and the Jewish people, his commands, his voice, but it is a very difficult thing to describe properly. One way of understanding the Torah is to say it is a gift. God gave it to the Jews, so it is taken very seriously. They believe it is the most important gift one could ever have.

Different views

Orthodox Jews believe that every word of the Torah as well as the traditional ways of interpreting it (the Oral Torah) were revealed by God. They do not question whether a law is still relevant, but study what it means and how they can put it into practice.

Other Jews believe the Torah was the work of a number of writers and gives general guidance about how God wants the Jewish people to behave, so some laws may be less relevant today than others. These Jews are called Liberal or Reform or sometimes **Progressive** Jews.

A middle way is held by Conservative Jews. They may accept that the Torah was not revealed at one moment in time, but believe that the traditional interpretations of it are inspired by God and that Jews can choose the most suitable. They believe change should be more gradual.

ASSIGNMENTS

● Look up this quotation from the Torah: Exodus 20:12. Write
an interpretation of it, explaining its meaning and how it
applies to life today. Compare your interpretations around
the class and discuss the similarities and differences. Try to
find one interpretation you can all agree on.

● Do some research into the different customs of the three
religious groupings mentioned here. Take one aspect,
such as how they observe Shabbat, dietary laws, or
synagogue worship, and write a dialogue between two Jews
of different groups in which they describe and explain their
different practices to each other. Try to link their practices
to their beliefs about the Torah.

KEY WORDS

Torah   Orthodox   Progressive

These Torah scrolls were attacked and damaged in
1939 by the Nazis

ISRAEL THE LAND

Where do you feel at home?

● Discuss where you feel most at home and what makes that place a home to you. List a few of the things that seem most important about it and share these with a partner if you wish.

One reason why Israel is the place where many Jews feel at home comes from the Torah. In the book of Genesis, Abraham is described as the patriarch or father of the Jewish people. But Abraham was not born in Israel, he was led to it and given it by God. The Torah describes how and why this happened:

God said to Abraham, 'Leave your home and go to the land I will show you and I will make you a great nation'. . . . So Abraham went . . . and came to Canaan . . . and God appeared to Abraham and said, 'I will give this land to your descendants.'

[Genesis 12:1–7]

How do Jews feel about Israel today?

Today Jewish feeling about Israel as a homeland is very strong. Since the end of the nineteenth century some Jews felt it was necessary to have a country of their own and that the land given to Abraham seemed rightfully theirs. Those who wanted to create a Jewish state there were called Zionists and their movement **Zionism** after Mount Zion, a mountain in Jerusalem. But long before Zionism grew up Jews had always prayed that one day they could again live freely in the land of Israel. As a sign of this, Jews all over the world face Jerusalem when they pray.

When the Falashas, black Ethiopian Jews, were suffering from famine during the 1980s, the State of Israel brought them to safety by flying them to a new home in Israel. Here is how one Israeli welcomed them:

I became a Zionist on the day I fled with my mother from the Budapest ghetto and there was nowhere for us to hide. They wanted to kill us and in the whole world there was nowhere for us to go. We had to return to the ghetto, but since then I have known that there has to be a place somewhere on the face of the earth which can offer haven to a Jewish child whose life is threatened by Nazis or by famine. In one sentence that is what Zionism is. Welcome my black brothers. You are helping us understand what we are doing here.

Many Jews feel that Israel is the place where they can be Jews most comfortably. It is the only place where Jews are not a minority.

ASSIGNMENTS

● Read Genesis 12:1–7. List the important things that Abraham is told about the land of Israel. Briefly explain why this makes Israel a very special place for Jews.

● You are asked to produce a leaflet explaining why some Jews wish to go and live in Israel when they already live somewhere else. Include all the important reasons you can find, mentioning also the possible disadvantages.

KEY WORDS

Zionism

An Israeli settlement in the Negev desert

THE COMING OF THE MESSIAH

● What would your ideal world be like? Share a song, picture or idea that you have about an ideal world and discuss the most important things it says.

Is the world getting worse or better?

A new world

For Jews the ideal world will come with the **Messianic Age**. This is the time when God will send the **Messiah** to put the world right. The word 'messiah' means 'anointed one', that is, one whom God has chosen. They believe the biblical prophets were inspired by God to tell of his coming. One of the greatest prophets was Isaiah, who said this (11:1–9):

> And there shall grow up a descendant from the family of David and the spirit of . . . wisdom and understanding . . . good sense and power . . . and knowledge of God shall be upon him. His judgements will not be based on outward impressions but he will judge the poor and the humble folk with fairness and virtue . . . Wolves will live with lambs and leopards with baby goats and little children shall shepherd them. . . . Lions will eat vegetation only, babies will play safely around snakes' nests. No one shall do harm in all of my holy places for the whole world will be enveloped in knowledge of God.

When will the Messiah come?

Jews believe that the Messiah will come for one of two reasons. Either the world will get better and be ready for the Messiah or it will get worse and need the Messiah to put it right. Here are two different Jewish opinions about this:

> 'The time is now ripe for the coming of the Mashiakh [Messiah]. Israel is in existence after 2,000 years of trying, and more young Jews are turning to true Torah principles, and the world is at last caring about universal things like human rights.'
>
> 'We live in a world so full of depravity and terror, that we are obviously coming to the end of days. The collapse of the environment and the threat to the whole of mankind means that the Mashiakh must come soon.'

ASSIGNMENTS

● By trying to interpret what Isaiah said and by looking at the picture, explain how the world will be different when the Messiah comes. Write a piece of prose or draw a picture to represent this.

● You have been asked to present a television programme on whether the world is ready for, or in need of, the Messiah. With a partner, collect material from newspapers and other sources to illustrate your view. Write a script, to go with this material, for your programme. You may wish to record this on tape, in the form of a debate about whether the Messiah is about to come.

KEY WORDS

Messianic Age   Messiah

THE JUSTICE OF GOD

Is God just?

● Look at the list of words below. Which of them do you think are important to the idea of justice? Compare your list with others in the class and discuss similarities and differences: fairness, goodness, mercy, equality, freedom, law, truth, punishment, reward.

It is quite common for Jews to talk of God as a judge. One of the earliest examples of this is in the story of Abraham, the first Jew, who challenged God when God told him that he intended to wipe out the two wicked cities of Sodom and Gomorrah (Genesis 18:23–32). Abraham argued with God with the words: 'Will not the judge of all the world do justly?'

Can we judge God?

While it seems right to ask Jews to be just, it also looks as if God is often unjust. Good people suffer and bad people prosper.

In Poland during the Second World War the Jews trapped in the Warsaw Ghetto were so devastated by their experiences that they decided to put God on trial. After presenting the evidence for and against God, the time had come for the judgement to be pronounced. The man playing the part of Judge found God guilty of dreadful injustice. As he was pondering what sentence to pass, someone pointed out that it was time to say the afternoon service and so they left off from the trial and turned to their prayers.

ASSIGNMENTS

● Read Genesis 18:23–32 and, after careful class discussion, draw up a list of four statements saying what this story seems to be teaching Jews about God, how God behaves, how God wants people to behave, and what is the ideal relationship between God and people. Compare your statements with others in the class and discuss any differences. Write up your conclusions.

● Read about King Solomon's judgement in the case of the two mothers (1 Kings 3:16–28). Imagine you were a reporter at the occasion when Solomon gave his judgement. Write an article for the front page of your paper explaining what happened and why you think Solomon made the judgement he gave. Consider whether it was a good judgement from a Jewish viewpoint. The headline you choose should reflect your opinion.

● It was obviously possible for the Jews in the Warsaw Ghetto to judge God but also worship him. Imagine you were one of those Jews and explain how you felt in a diary entry of the event. Discuss with a partner a situation in your own life with, for example, your father, mother or a friend, when you would feel similarly.

A fifteenth-century illustration of the Judgement of Solomon

PESAKH

Most people have several 'new years'. For example, we register our cars from August, we organise our tax affairs from April and we reopen our schools in September. Judaism also has several New Years. Each one celebrates a different aspect of the world and life as Jews understand them.

● Think of a ceremony you do at a New Year celebration and explain it to a partner in as much detail as you can, including the reason why you do it. Notice what you and your partner's ceremonies have in common and how they are different.

The birthday of the Jewish people

Pesakh celebrates the birthday of the Jewish people and falls in the first month of the Jewish year, in springtime. It commemorates the most important event in their history: freedom from slavery in Egypt more than three thousand years ago – the **Exodus**.

● Read this story in the book of Exodus (chapters 12 and 13) and notice who it was that led them out of Egypt. Discuss and write a brief explanation of what you think the word 'Exodus' means to a Jew and why the festival that celebrates it is called Pesakh, meaning 'passover'.

The point for the Jews is not that Moses led them out of Egypt but that *God* did. When Jews commemorate the Exodus from Egypt on the evening of Pesakh, they do not actually mention Moses at all.

The Seder

Jews particularly celebrate this Exodus at the **Seder**, a special meal and service conducted at home on the eve of Pesakh, which is actually a week-long festival. At this ceremony, the story of the Exodus is told in as interesting a way as possible. A number of symbolic foods are eaten during the service. Some of these items are displayed on a special plate called a Seder dish. Also on the table are salt water, wine and **matza**. Besides a taste of these symbolic foods there is also a full-scale feast in the middle of the telling of the story. At the end of the Seder, because it is a happy event, there are many songs to be sung. One of these is a song called 'Who knows One?' Here is the last verse set to the tune of 'Green Grow the Rushes Oh'.

Who knows what thirteen are,
now our Seder's finishing?
I know what thirteen are:
Thirteen virtues God displays,
Twelve are the tribes of Israel,
Eleven are the stars in Joseph's dream,
Ten are the commandments,
Nine are the months of pregnancy,
Eight is the day to circumcise,
Seven are the days in ev'ry week,
Six are the sections of Mishna,
Five are the books of the Torah,

Four are the People's mothers,
Three are the fathers of the Jews,
Two are the stones of Law on which the
    Cov'nant's given,
One is God for evermore on earth and
    up in heaven.

Pesakh remembers the suffering and
celebrates the freedom. It also looks
forward to the Messianic Age when
everyone will be truly free.

A Seder plate

ASSIGNMENTS

● Read or sing the last verse of the Seder song. Research and
carefully explain what each of the thirteen items refers to
and why these are so important to Jews.

● Look at the picture. Research what the items are on the
Seder plate to which the people are pointing. Imagine you
are at the meal and have to tell the story of the Exodus. Tell
the story in as interesting and entertaining a way as you can
(remember there will be children around the table) and
explain the meaning of the Seder plate and the items.

KEY WORDS

Pesakh   Exodus   Seder   matza

ROSH HASHANA

The birthday of the world

The Torah describes the creation of the world in the book of Genesis. There are many ways of understanding this story but it does say that there was one moment when the world was created. It is from this moment that Jews count their years, so that it is now the 58th century. 1991/92, for example, in the Jewish calendar is 5752. Very few Jews believe that the world was created exactly this number of years ago. Nevertheless, by using this number they show that they want to see history as a whole and not just the history of one particular people or religion.

While Pesakh celebrates the birthday of the Jewish people, **Rosh Hashana** celebrates the birthday of the world. It falls in the seventh month of the Jewish year in September or October and lasts for 48 hours. For Jews, this is when the year number changes and God starts a review of the behaviour of every human being. So on Rosh Hashana Jews also try to review and improve their behaviour. This is usually called repenting, which means being truly sorry. The Hebrew word 'teshuva' really means 'returning'. This implies that people are basically good and can return to their original pleasant relationship with God. At this time Jews particularly think of the story in Genesis about God's test of Abraham, when God asked him to sacrifice his son Isaac.

'At last, after nineteen centuries,
the Jewish people have finally come home' –
Colonel in Israeli Army, June 1967

The shofar

The **shofar** is the horn of any kosher animal but the most commonly used is that of a ram. A legend says the horns of the ram in the story of Abraham and Isaac were taken up to heaven. One was used for the trumpet blast at the giving of the Ten Commandments and the other is reserved for the trumpet blast which will announce the Messianic Age. Chief Rabbi Goren blew the shofar when the Western Wall of the Temple in Jerusalem was recaptured in 1967 after 2,000 years of Jewish exile.

ASSIGNMENTS

● Read the story of Abraham and Isaac in Genesis 22:1–18 and imagine yourself at a gathering where you have to explain the meaning of Rosh Hashana for Jews. Using the story as your guide, write a talk for this occasion.

● In Jerusalem in 1967 the fighting was particularly dangerous because the Israeli authorities did not want to use shells and artillery for fear of damaging the holy sites. Imagine you were a soldier who fought his way through the streets to the Western Wall. Now you are standing watching the shofar being blown, celebrating Rosh Hashana in Jerusalem for the first time. Describe your thoughts and feelings, remembering your experiences and thinking about the meaning of Jewish New Year. (You may find it helpful to reread pages 10–11 about the Messiah before doing this assignment.)

KEY WORDS

Rosh Hashana   shofar

YOM KIPPUR

A nineteenth-century painting of Yom Kippur
in a Polish synagogue

Yom Kippur is the most important day in the Jewish year. In Hebrew it is also called Shabbat Shabbaton, 'the most important Shabbat'. It is the simplest and starkest festival in the Jewish year. Everything ceremonial is white, because white on Yom Kippur reminds Jews of shrouds and therefore mortality. It is also the colour of purity – the High Priest wore simple white linen on Yom Kippur.

Yom Kippur is the Day of **Atonement**. It ends the ten days started by Rosh Hashana and finalises the yearly programme of **teshuva** (repentance). On this day, Jews imagine God as if he were sitting with a huge accounting book, totting up what each person deserves, based on what they have done and on the sincerity of what they intend to do. It is a day on which Jews become very conscious of how frail they are – not eating or drinking for a day makes you realise that human beings are not as great as they sometimes think they are.

Leaving the world

The day is spent in synagogue, no food or drink is consumed, no work is done. Everything seems stripped bare, down to the absolute essentials. One effect of this is that by the end you really do leave the outside world behind, whereas if you just visit for a morning or afternoon service, you very quickly get back to the world outside with all the distractions of television, work and so on. A Jewish teenager explained his attitude to Yom Kippur:

'I suppose I really go to shul [synagogue] on Yom Kippur to be with my friends. They all go too. I'm not very religious but I wouldn't dream of not fasting on Yom Kippur. I spend most of the day outside shul chatting but I don't do that on Kol Nidre [the eve of Yom Kippur, a two-hour service] and during the day I stay in for about an hour and a half in the morning and I make sure I'm back for Neila [the concluding service of about one and a half hours]. I'm not sure why I do it. My parents want me to and you sort of feel better at the end of the day. In a way it sets you up for the year but it's hell catching up with the school work. No one at school seems to make allowances. They think it's a holiday!'

ASSIGNMENTS

● Look at the painting of Jews in a synagogue on Yom Kippur. Imagine you were at this occasion and describe and explain it in a letter to someone who wants to know what it is like. Remember that this occasion is a time of repentance. Try to help the person reading your letter understand what that means.

● Imagine you are a Jew writing an article about Yom Kippur for a Sunday magazine. Research and describe the distinctive practices of Yom Kippur and give reasons for them. Explain why it is the most widely observed Jewish festival. Draw a picture that might illustrate the article.

KEY WORDS

Yom Kippur   Atonement   teshuva

SHABBAT

Shabbat is a weekly day of celebration for Jews when God commands that they keep a 'holy day of rest'.

● If you had to spend a 'holy day of rest', what exactly would you do or not do? Jot down the different ways in which you use your leisure time and then discuss with two or three others if you could still do these things and, if not, what you should do instead.

You may have found it difficult to decide what you mean by 'holy' and 'rest'. Jews have the same problem with the fourth Commandment (Exodus 20:8–11), which tells them to keep Shabbat holy and to do no work.

What is forbidden?

Traditionally, to help decide what is forbidden on Shabbat, Jews look back to the most important work they had to do in the desert after the Exodus from Egypt. This was the making of the Sanctuary for God. Despite the importance of this task the Israelites stopped work on it every Shabbat. Guided by this it seems every job involved in this task must be forbidden. These were listed as 39 types of work:

Ploughing, sowing, reaping, sheaf-making, threshing, winnowing, selecting, sifting, grinding, kneading, baking, sheep-shearing, bleaching, combing raw material, dyeing, spinning, threading a loom, weaving, removing the cloth, separating threads, tying a knot, untying it, sewing, tearing, trapping, slaughtering, skinning, tanning, scraping, marking, cutting a shape, writing, erasing, building, demolishing, lighting a fire, putting it out, striking the last hammer blow, carrying in a public place.

Orthodox Jews believe this traditional understanding of what is forbidden is important because it means all Jews know exactly what they can and can't do. Progressive Jews say it is the principle of resting that is important. This keeps a day holy, rather than exactly what you do and don't do.

What is commanded?

Besides what you *can* do, you must decide what you *should* do to make a day holy. Jewish tradition requires praising God (with a community where possible), reading Torah, enjoying three meals, singing, studying and chatting. Shabbat is a social feast day. Here is what Shabbat means to one Jewish parent:

'I can't think of anything that makes us feel more like a family than Shabbat together. Every week we all spend a whole day together – and not just any day but a special festival day with wine and all our best things out and time to play and three good meals round the table all together at the same time.'

Shabbat eve in Israel

ASSIGNMENTS

● One half of the class should think as Orthodox Jews and, from the list of 39 kinds of work, list everyday things they could still do. The other half should think as Progressive Jews and list what they would do on Shabbat. Compare your lists and discuss reasons for the similarities and differences. Write a report on how and why the groups differed.

● What is happening in the picture? Research what happens at a Shabbat meal and write an explanation of this scene for someone who knows nothing about Shabbat.

KEY WORDS

Shabbat

HANUKA

The story of Hanuka

Hanuka celebrates an event which took place about 160 years before the events Christmas commemorates, at a time when the Syrian Greeks had taken over the **Temple** in Jerusalem and were trying to force the Jews to give up their religion. A family called the **Maccabees** led a revolt which enabled them to win back control of the Temple and some independence. Hanuka celebrates the rededication of the Temple. ('Hanuka' means dedication.) As a result, throughout the ages, Hanuka has served as a kind of beacon and reminder to the Jews that it is not impossible to defeat a large and powerful enemy if you believe strongly enough in the justness of your cause.

As part of the rededication of the Temple the Everlasting Light had to be relit. According to the story, a pot of oil

The centre candle is the servant that lights the other eight on a hanukia

which would allow the lamp to burn for only one day miraculously lasted for eight, giving the Jews time to make more and keep the lamp burning. At Hanuka, to commemorate this, an eight-branched candlestick is lit, with one extra candle being lit each evening until all eight are burning.

Hanuka and Christmas

The Festival of Hanuka has become very popular in recent years, even though it is not really a very important festival. One reason for this popularity is that, as Jews started to be allowed to mix in a Christian world, they needed to find something for their children to celebrate at Christmas time. However, this has also created some difficulties for the Jewish community as these two Jews explain:

'I always find Hanuka time the most challenging with my children. They're surrounded by Christmas at school, in the streets and on TV. Somehow I have to help them not to mind that it's all nothing to do with us and that they're not going to get stockings and turkey and all that. We have the custom of giving little presents every night of Hanuka so that makes it last the whole eight days instead of one big noise then nothing. And actually the whole story about the few in the face of the many and one little pot of oil outlasting people's expectations seems to fit particularly well when I'm trying to get the children to think about not just going along with the Christmas thing just because everyone else is doing it.'

'When we first came to England in 1975 from Iraq we didn't make much of a fuss of Hanuka. It's only a minor festival. Back in Baghdad we did give presents and of course we lit the **hanukia** every night and so on. We had special fried foods at Hanuka, like little sweet cakes, but mostly it was a chance to give to charity rather than just presents to people who didn't need them. We certainly never had Hanuka cards! I think that's just aping Christmas. Jews should be more proud to do their own thing, not just imitate other people.'

ASSIGNMENTS

● You have been asked to explain the story of Hanuka to the children in the picture. Research and write the story as you would tell it to them, explaining the meaning of the candles and why it is important for them to remember it.

● Imagine you are a Jewish parent whose child wants to know why she doesn't get lots of presents on Christmas Day like other children. Tape or write down your explanation to her of why this is and explain what you have decided to do at Hanuka to help with this situation.

KEY WORDS

Hanuka   Temple   Maccabees
hanukia

RITES OF PASSAGE

WELCOME TO THE WORLD

When a Jewish woman gives birth, her baby is a Jew. Immediately the child becomes a link in the chain of the Jewish people, a chain stretching back over thousands of years. Obviously, Jews hope the link will be a strong one. The arrival of a child is an event to be celebrated. The chain of the Jewish people will be continued.

Boy or girl?

All over the world, the first thing announced about a birth is whether the baby is a boy or a girl. For Jews, a new birth is an occasion for joy, regardless of whether the baby is male or female, but the way a Jewish birth is celebrated depends on the gender of the baby.

● Discuss as a group whether you imagine you will have any preferences about the gender of your children. What different kinds of reasons do you have for your decision?

Welcoming girls

At the first opportunity after a girl is born, her father is called to a reading of the Torah at the Shabbat service to announce her name. So within a week of her birth she is welcomed into the community. (If she does not have a Jewish father someone else can do this.)

Welcoming boys

When a boy is eight days old, the ceremony of **circumcision** takes place. The Bible says that God told Abraham that, when his son Isaac was eight days old, he should circumcise his penis. This means the foreskin is cut away. This is a sign of the covenant, or relationship, which exists between God and the Jewish people. In Hebrew the 'Covenant of Circumcision' is called **Brit Mila**, so a circumcision is often just called a 'Brit'. The ceremony often takes place at home and is performed by a **mohel** – a circumciser – who is often also a rabbi.

From the moment of birth, Judaism recognises that there are important differences between girls and boys. A Jewish Marriage Guidance Counsellor explained:

'There are not just physical differences between men and women but also emotional and spiritual ones. Girls tend to be more sensitive and social, while boys are more competitive. Judaism tries to play to these strengths and there is no point in forcing women to do things to make them more spiritual when they are more spiritual already. Just look at any religion, not just Judaism. It's the women who keep it going.'

ASSIGNMENTS

● The picture shows a circumcision ceremony taking place. Imagine the thoughts of the various people in the picture – some of whom are probably related to the baby. Write down your ideas and exchange your thoughts with others in the group.

● Someone has suggested that boys seem to be more important than girls in Judaism. Research this issue more fully and then write a dialogue in which you explain why this is or is not a misunderstanding.

● What views do you have about the final quote from the marriage counsellor? Write down some questions and points you might want to make if you met her. Discuss the ideas in a group.

KEY WORDS

circumcision   Brit Mila   mohel

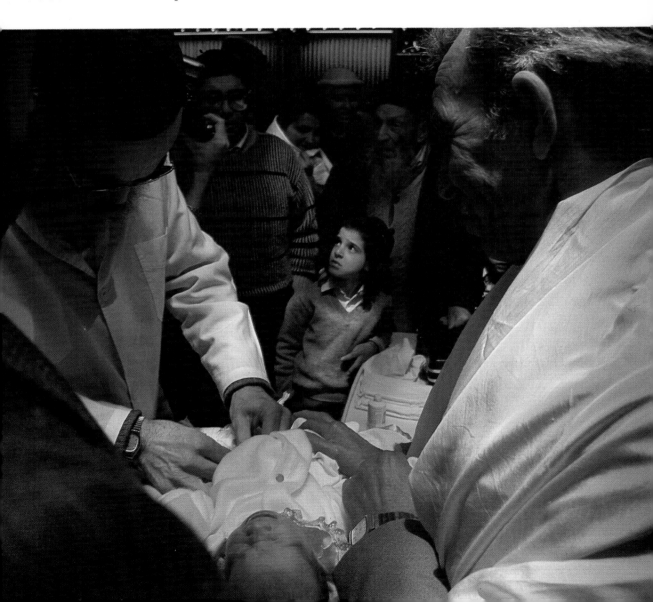

BATMITZVAH AND BARMITZVAH

When are we adults?

● Discuss the following questions:
What is an adult?
At what age do you think adulthood begins?
When does the law in Britain recognise someone as an adult?

The Torah says that at 21 Jews are ready to fight for their country, pay taxes and be responsible in law. However, in Jewish tradition, a girl takes on religious responsibilities at the age of 12 and boys at the age of 13. For girls the occasion is called **Batmitzvah** (daughter of the

commandments). For boys it is called **Barmitzvah** (son of the commandments).

The ceremony is a major event in a Jewish person's life. A 13-year-old boy from Glasgow explained his feelings on the day of his Barmitzvah:

'I had been having extra lessons for a year with my rabbi but I was still dreadfully nervous when I went up to the **bima** to read my piece. I took a deep breath and sang as loud as I could. Slowly it became easier somehow and I relaxed a bit. When I had finished, I could see everyone congratulating my dad and I looked up and all the women, Mum and everyone, looked proud of me. I was really pleased I hadn't let anyone down and now I could look forward to tomorrow's party and all the presents I hoped to get.'

When boys and girls reach these ages they are expected to fast on Yom Kippur, drink the four cups of wine on Pesakh and generally not blame anyone else but themselves for their behaviour.

A controversial area

In the 1800s, Liberal Jews abolished Bar/ Batmitzvah. Instead they had a

This boy's Barmitzvah gift was a trip to Jerusalem where his Barmitzvah was celebrated at the Western Wall

Confirmation at 16. Many Liberal Jews now have a Bat/Barmitzvah at 12/13 and Confirmation at 16. These ceremonies create a great deal of discussion and disagreement. Two Jewish teenagers expressed their views:

'I'm pleased I had Confirmation at 16. It is a much more sensible age to take on board responsibility for your religious duties. At 13 I didn't really know what I thought and wasn't mature enough to make a proper commitment.'

'I'm pleased I didn't have a Batmitzvah. Having a ceremony is just imitating the boys and it's not necessary. As for Confirmation, I don't understand that. It's like having a ceremony to confirm that you're a girl. I think it's silly.'

ASSIGNMENTS

● Research more detail about what happens at Bat/Barmitzvah. Produce a script for a radio documentary about the ceremonies and include any ideas of your own about the idea of whether 12/13 seems to be the right age for an event like this.

● Look carefully at the picture. Imagine the boy sends a letter home to friends who could not make the trip to Jerusalem for the ceremony. Write the letter, imagining how he might describe his feelings about the experience.

KEY WORDS

Batmitzvah   Barmitzvah   bima

MARRIAGE AND LOVE

● Decide what qualities your partner for life would have. Discuss in a group how you intend to find that partner. How difficult do you imagine it will be to discover the *ideal* partner?

The Jewish approach

The Bible says that when Isaac married Rebecca 'he married her and he loved her'. The rabbis say that love is more important after a marriage than before it. It's not marrying the person you love that matters but loving the person you marry. Marriage in Judaism involves more than just the couple who are marrying. Families are coming together and it is important to keep up the historical chain of Judaism.

● The picture shows a wedding feast. Imagine the thoughts of the parents of the bride and groom as they look around at the guests. Write down these thoughts, remembering how important marriage is in maintaining the chain of Judaism.

'My parents said I should see her table manners. I refused two girls because I knew I could not spend the rest of my life watching them eat with their mouths open.'

'I know there are so many intelligent women who have let themselves go because they have fallen in love. I'm pleased there are wiser heads around me who helped me in my choice.'

Most Jews, however, like most other people in Britain, wander around hoping to bump into the right person. Judaism considers it a miracle that people succeed in this unlikely attempt. When a Roman asked a rabbi what God has done since creating the world, the rabbi answered, 'He has been making marriages.'

Arranged marriages

A minority of Jewish families still practise arranged marriages. The young people can refuse the partner who has been proposed, but they know their parents have experience, their own best interests at heart and a more balanced approach. These young people found their partners in this way:

Divorce

Technically divorce is easy in Judaism. Because marriage is a legal contract, it is possible to withdraw from it as long as both parties agree. No precise reason is needed for divorce, just that the marriage has collapsed beyond repair. But divorce is not viewed lightly. The Talmud says that God's altar weeps over every divorce.

ASSIGNMENTS

● Imagine you are a young Jew whose parents are proposing an arranged marriage, but you want to go out and find your own partner. Write an account of the conversation you have with your parents as you discuss the advantages and disadvantages of this system of finding a marriage partner.

● Research more information about the wedding ceremony and write a section which could be added to this book to explain the important details.

A wedding feast in Israel amongst Oriental Jews

DEATH AND MOURNING

If you were with a Jewish family just after someone had died it would seem that the aim is to bury the body in a dignified way, as quickly and simply as possible – and then turn to give help to those who are left to mourn.

When a Jew dies, the body is washed, then dressed or wrapped in plain linen and placed in a simple coffin. A male will also be wrapped in his tallit (the prayer shawl). The coffin is made of chipboard with a veneer and rope handles. The idea is to make the burial simple as a reminder that all who enter the world are born equal and that we should leave the world in the same way. No undertakers are employed. At the cemetery, all who are present shovel earth into the grave until it is more or less full. Burying the dead is a great mitzva, because it is the one mitzva for which you can get no thanks!

● Discuss the idea that a funeral should be kept as simple and straightforward as possible. Do you agree with this?

Mourning rites

Immediately after the funeral, the close family share a week of mourning called **Shiva**. They wear a torn garment and sit on low chairs to follow two passages in the Bible which speak of mourners tearing their clothes and being brought low in grief. They will not work, cook, watch television or try to distract themselves from the emotions of mourning. Jews believe it is important to focus all one's thoughts on the death which has occurred.

News of a death travels fast and friends will know that the family is now in mourning. They will offer support by taking food, doing the chores and offering sympathy. The synagogue services will be moved to the home of the family where the mourner's prayer, the **Kaddish**, will be said. Here is a passage from it:

> Magnified and sanctified be God's great name in the world which He has created as He wished. May He establish His kingdom during your life and days, and during the days of all the House of Israel, quickly and very soon, and say, Amen.

● The Kaddish prayer does not mention death. Why do you think the mourners say this prayer?

Death and mourning customs

Jews traditionally believe that on Judgement Day all souls will be rewarded according to their behaviour on earth. Most Jews do not think about this too much, and many are not sure what they believe about life after death.

In many cemeteries the bodies lie with their feet pointing towards Jerusalem. At the moment of resurrection they believe they will return to Jerusalem, the heart of the Jewish people. Mirrors are covered in the home during Shiva, possibly to discourage the mourners from vanity, and possibly because of an old tradition that a soul could return to life through a mirror. Orthodox Jews will not be cremated as they believe that they will be physically resurrected, but they do allow the use of transplants to save the lives of others.

A Jewish graveyard in Jerusalem

ASSIGNMENTS

● The features of death and mourning in Judaism reflect some basic Jewish beliefs. Read these two pages again and see how many ideas you can identify.

● The photograph shows a Jewish graveyard. Imagine you are a parent taking your son or daughter to this cemetery for the first time. Write a dialogue in which you answer the questions which you imagine the child might ask about Jewish practice.

● What is your reaction to the idea of a week of mourning? What value do you think there is in this practice? Discuss with others and write a piece explaining the different viewpoints.

KEY WORDS

Shiva   Kaddish

THE TORAH

The central point of any Shabbat service will be the reading from the Torah scroll. On Shabbat morning a section is read and, over the course of a year, the Torah will be completed. The festival of **Simkhat Torah** is the celebration of the day the reading is completed and started again.

The Torah is the first and most important part of the Jewish Bible or **Tenakh**. Because Jews believe the Torah is a gift from God, every detail of the text is carefully preserved. Writing the Torah in Hebrew on a scroll is a job which is highly valued in the Jewish community.

A Torah scroll is raised at the Western Wall

A 32-year-old scribe (**sofer**) from Jerusalem explained:

'I chose to become a sofer because it seemed to me to be the most important task. To be a mohel [circumciser] or a shokhet [kosher butcher] are secondary – without the Torah there would be no Jewish babies and no kosher meat. So I love to write Torah. I am doing a full scroll at the moment – that's about a year's work. Somehow in writing a scroll in exactly the same way as it has always been written, I feel like I am helping to bring the Torah down from Mount Sinai to the Jews.'

A perfect text

Ensuring that no mistake ever creeps into the text is crucial for Jews. This experience illustrates the point:

'One week in shul while reading from the Torah, our rabbi suddenly stopped in mid-sentence. He looked around and beckoned to a boy who must have been 12 – his Barmitzvah was to happen in the following month. The boy went forward to the reading desk, there was a conversation and, the next thing I knew, they were putting the scroll aside and taking another from the Ark. The rabbi had spotted a letter which had become faint with age. Since the young boy, who should know the letters, couldn't say for sure what the letter was, the scroll was immediately declared non-kosher until it could be repaired. If you continue to use a non-kosher scroll and mistakes begin to creep in, the Jewish faith is under threat.'

When a Torah scroll is so badly damaged that it can't be repaired – by fire for example – it is buried with the same simplicity and respect as the human body is given, in a proper cemetery. After all, it's not easy to decide which is more valuable or more perfectly God's creation.

ASSIGNMENTS

● A friend tells you he doesn't understand why Jews don't just have a Torah book, produced like any other, rather than employ scribes to produce handwritten scrolls. It would be far more efficient. Write your reply from a Jewish point of view.

● Reread the last passage about what happens to a scroll of Torah when it cannot be repaired, and look at the picture of the desecrated scrolls on page 7. Produce a radio programme which gives a Jewish reaction to the event shown in the picture. Do some research then choose suitable introductory music and use your imagination to provide quotations from newspapers of the time. Interview an eyewitness looking back at the event and provide commentary by an expert on the subject. Two people could act as presenters of the programme and link it together.

KEY WORDS

Simkhat Torah   Tenakh   sofer

NEVI'IM

The Torah is not the only portion of the Jewish scriptures read on Shabbat. **Nevi'im** is a collection of writings from the prophets which Jews believe to have been inspired by God – although they are not as central to the religion as the Torah. This is the second part of the Tenakh.

Using Nevi'im

The name of Israel's airline, EL AL, is taken from a passage in Nevi'im in the book of Ezekiel. Ezekiel speaks of a time in the future when all Jews will be gathered up to return to Israel and he uses the phrase 'el al' which means 'flying forward'. So the prophets even live on in a modern airline.

Readings from Nevi'im are usually used to echo ideas which have appeared in the weekly reading from the Torah. Nevi'im is used as a kind of dialogue with the Torah. It can also be used on special occasions to give added meaning to an important event. For example, at every wedding, Jeremiah 33:11 is read:

Soon the sounds of joy and gladness shall be heard in Judean cities again, the voices of brides and bridegrooms.

In this way the passage from the Prophets is used to suggest that every wedding is a sign of the hope of the coming Messianic Age. Similarly, when leaving a graveyard after a funeral, Jews wash their hands and say these words from Isaiah 25:8:

He will destroy death for ever; the Lord God will wipe away tears from every face and will remove from all the earth all insults against his people.

In this way, times of sadness also look forward to the coming Messianic Age when mourning will be no more.

The authority of Nevi'im

While Nevi'im is not as authoritative as the Torah, many important Jewish practices are based on its guidance. For example, on every Shabbat in Britain, a prayer is said for the Royal Family. In other countries it's for the President or the Parliament. This is based on Jeremiah 29:7:

Seek the welfare of any city to which you have been carried off and pray to God on its behalf, because your peace depends on its welfare.

Jewish ex-servicemen and women hold their Armistice Day Parade at the Cenotaph in Whitehall, London

ASSIGNMENTS

● Reread Jeremiah 29:7 and discuss why you think this passage has inspired the saying of prayers for a nation's leaders. Describe a situation in which a Jew might find it difficult to abide by this passage from Nevi'im.

● Think of three or four other occasions that, as a Jew, you might wish to mark by quoting from Nevi'im (e.g. the birth of a child or a homewarming). In groups choose one of the books of Nevi'im and research quotations for the occasion. Discuss your findings as a class and decide which quotations you would wish to use. Write up one of your quotations, explaining what occasion it is for and why you chose it.

● The photograph shows Jewish ex-servicemen and women holding their own Armistice Parade at the Cenotaph in Whitehall, London, in November. They also take part in the main ceremony. Using the quotation from Jeremiah, write a short commentary on the photograph from the point of view of a Jewish participant.

KEY WORDS

Nevi'im

KETUVIM

Ketuvim makes up the final part of the Tenakh. It is more poetic than Nevi'im and includes the psalms and books like Esther and Ruth. Orthodox Jews read eight psalms at the beginning of the daily morning service and 16 at the beginning of the Shabbat morning service.

The selection of psalms to be read by the community is done very carefully. They express many different experiences and are chosen to reflect the mood of any occasion. Particular psalms are recommended for reading when you move into a new home, when someone is sick, when someone is about to give birth or when burying the dead. The following verses from Psalm 102 are read on Holocaust Day when the Jews recall the horrors of their treatment in the concentration and death camps of Nazi Europe:

> Hide not your face from me when I am in trouble, listen to me when I call, and answer me speedily. For my days are swallowed up like smoke and my bones are burnt like a hearth ... my bones stick to my skin ... my enemies insult me all day ... all I have eaten is ashes like bread.

● Discuss why this passage is particularly appropriate for Holocaust Day. What feelings do you imagine the psalm might convey?

The festival of Purim
in a synagogue in Jerusalem

A quarry for new prayers

Judaism is not a static religion. When a special occasion arises or when new circumstances face the Jewish community, they will search in Ketuvim to find appropriate passages to read. It is as if the Jewish people feel they are in a constantly renewed conversation with God through the passages of the Bible.

With the return of the Jews to Jerusalem many of these ancient psalms suddenly seem very up to date again. Nothing much seems to have changed in the Middle East over the last two or three thousand years!

ASSIGNMENTS

● The following psalms are read on particular occasions. Read at least two of the psalms and try to match them up with the appropriate occasion:
Psalm 22, Psalm 91, Psalm 112, Psalm 122.
When collecting for charity.
When going on a journey.
When at home on Shabbat afternoon.
What reasons would you give for the choices you have made?

● The photograph shows the festival of Purim being celebrated in a synagogue in Jerusalem. Describe what you see. This festival is derived from the book of Esther. Read the book of Esther and suggest on what sort of occasions it could prove a valuable source of guidance for Jews.

KEY WORDS

Ketuvim

TALMUD

Over the centuries the Jewish people have debated and argued about many different aspects of their faith. These debates and ideas have been collected together into an encyclopaedia of Jewish wisdom known as the **Talmud**, in which different views on many matters are written down. However, the Talmud doesn't tell you what to think. It provides guidance and is a source of much discussion among Jews today.

● Every culture has its own selection of stories, proverbs and anecdotes which provide guidance and wisdom for each new generation. What examples can you think of from your own culture which provide you with a kind of Talmud?

A page from the Talmud. The centre of the page is the Talmud itself. The rest are traditional commentaries

The Mishna

The core of the Talmud is the **Mishna**. In the second century CE the Jewish people were being scattered all over the known world. Rabbi Judah, known as the Prince, was concerned that Jewish wisdom would be lost as the community was dispersed. He collected together a summary of the main points of the Oral Torah in a volume which became known as the Mishna. 'Mishna' means 'repetition', which makes the important point that Rabbi Judah was not adding anything new but simply recording the tradition in written form.

Aggada

Some of the material in the Talmud is known as **Aggada**. These are traditional stories which add to the collection of Jewish wisdom. Here is one of them:

When Moses asked God why the letters of the Torah were decorated he received the reply that one day a great rabbi called Akiva would be able to interpret the decoration even though Moses could not understand it. Moses asked if he could meet Rabbi Akiva. In a flash he was sitting in Akiva's classroom. Moses could not follow the discussion. One of Akiva's students asked him about some point in the Torah. Akiva replied that it had been given to Moses on Sinai. Moses was impressed that the Rabbi seemed to know more about the Torah than he did himself, even though he had received it on the mountain. Moses asked God, 'This man is truly great. Why did you give the Torah to me when you could have given it to Akiva who understands it much better?' God replied, 'Be silent, it is my decision.' So Moses then said, 'Having seen this great teacher, can I see the reward he received for his wisdom?' Moses then saw Akiva being tortured and burnt by the Romans. Moses challenged God, distressed at the injustice of the way Akiva was being treated. God replied, 'Be quiet. It is my decision.'

● What points do you think this story is trying to make? Discuss the ideas with others and decide what questions might be asked about the story.

ASSIGNMENTS

● It is sometimes suggested that Judaism is a religion which has fixed laws and is not flexible. How does the idea of the Talmud help to show this suggestion is inaccurate? Write a short piece to explain your ideas.

● It is a tradition among Jews to argue and discuss important points about their belief and practice. Some might feel that this is dangerous as religious people should be sure about what they believe. Discuss this as a class and decide whether you think certainty or questioning is the best quality for a religious believer. Write a report of this discussion giving your own point of view.

KEY WORDS

Talmud   Mishna   Aggada

THE SIDDUR AND THE SHEMA

Siddur means 'order'. It is also the name for the Jewish prayer book which sets out the order for the services, such as the grace before and after meals, the Shabbat services, the festival celebrations, and the various events in a Jew's life like Barmitzvah.

For example, the Shabbat service is carried out according to a set pattern, or liturgy. There is little space for people to make up their own prayers. The idea behind the pattern is that the prayers which are used can be applied to all situations. So the congregation will seek to find how the prayers relate to their situation rather than make up their own.

The Shema

At the heart of the Siddur and Jewish life is one prayer which is the most important

Blessings at the start of a meal

single thing a Jew will ever say. It is said at every morning and evening service and is often the first prayer a Jewish child will learn. It is recommended as the prayer to be said at the deathbed of a Jew. The prayer is known as the **Shema**.

The Shema is a long prayer made up of three sections from the Torah. This is the opening section (Deuteronomy 6:4–9):

> Listen Israel, the Lord is our God, the Lord is One. And you shall love the Lord your God with all your heart and with all your soul and with all your might. And these words, which I command you today, shall be upon your heart. And you shall teach these words carefully to your children, repeating them when you sit at home, when you walk in the street, when you go to bed and when you get up. And you shall tie these words as a sign upon your hand and they shall be placed on your forehead between your eyes. And you shall write these words on the doorposts of your house and on your gates.

The first two sentences of the prayer are the heart of the Jewish faith. The life of a Jew is an attempt to live out the full meaning of these words. The prayer suggests a number of ways in which Jews might try to keep these words at the centre of their lives.

● Identify at least five ways in which the prayer suggests a Jew might learn how to remember these words.

A Jewish father explained the importance of the Shema:

> 'Among the bedtime nursery rhymes we sing with our 22-month-old daughter is the Shema. I can't tell you my joy and pride the first time little Anna sang the first couple of words with me one evening as I was putting her to bed. These words will be with her all her life. The next day, as I do every year, I suggested to my Jewish GCSE pupils that they start each exam by saying the Shema before looking at the paper. It calms everything down. My wife did exactly the same last week when taking her final degree exams. And my mum, who's 70, always says the Shema when they set out to drive up and visit us.'

ASSIGNMENTS

● What is the most important single thing you could ever say? Sit silently for a moment and repeat to yourself any words which come to mind. What might be the importance of repeating these words to yourself every day? Write about how this has helped you to understand why repeating the Shema is important for Jews.

● 'What are scriptures for?' You have been asked to do a presentation, with this title, on Jewish scriptures. Read back over this section on Scriptures (pages 32–41) and research further if you need to. Construct a plan for your presentation putting down what you would say and what quotations and books or objects you would use.

KEY WORDS

Siddur   Shema

GETTING IN THE MOOD

Have you ever been in a situation, perhaps an assembly, when someone said, 'Let us pray' or 'Shall we spend a few minutes thinking about. . .'? You may have found it difficult to concentrate. Perhaps you were not in the mood. You may have had something else on your mind. If like Jews you have daily services which should be said at particular times of the day, how can you be sure that you will be in the mood at the right time?

Tefillin

The boy in the photograph is wearing **tefillin**, a distinctive practice of Judaism. The word 'tefillin' means 'prayers'. A set of tefillin consists of the **shel rosh** for the head and the **shel yad** for the hand and arm. Each is a box about three centimetres cubed and made from a fine kosher leather. Attached to each box is a long leather strap about one centimetre wide and painted with a glossy black surface. They are worn by men (males over 13) during weekday morning services. The act of putting on tefillin helps the men prepare, or 'get in the mood', for prayer.

Traditionally women do not wear tefillin because they do not need to say set services. However, in some Conservative synagogues some women might wear tefillin along with the men.

Orthodox Jews say that women do not need set services or reminders like tefillin because they are naturally more spiritual and in touch with God.

Heart and mind

Inside each box are four paragraphs in Hebrew from the Torah: the first two portions of the Shema (Deuteronomy 6:4–9 and 11:13–21); Exodus 13:1–10, and Exodus 13:11–16. The boxes appear similar but they are different. The shel rosh is divided into four compartments and each text is on a separate piece of parchment, put in separately. The shel yad is a single cube and inside it the four texts are written on one continuous piece of parchment.

Great care is taken when hand writing the parchment scrolls as tefillin are one of Judaism's few sacred items. Each one is an important symbol of faith in God. The shel rosh reminds the Jew that he must always serve God with his mind. The shel yad, bound on the upper biceps of the weaker arm, reminds the Jew to serve God with his heart and actions.

Tefillin are not worn on festivals because the rabbis say that Shabbat and festivals are also signs of God's relationship with the Jews so no other sign is required.

Praying at the Western Wall

ASSIGNMENTS

● Reread the passage from the Shema and what the Jewish father says about it on page 41. Now imagine you are the boy in the picture. Explain what you are wearing, doing and thinking at this moment.

● 'What's the use of prayer anyway?' Give an answer to this question from a Jewish point of view using the information here and on the Shema (page 41). Include your own ideas also.

KEY WORDS

tefillin   shel rosh   shel yad

HOME IS WHERE THE SOUL IS

Without a doubt, the home is the main place of Jewish practice. Not only is Judaism very much a family religion but there are many commandments or mitzvot (singular – **mitzva**) that are fulfilled in the home.

● Look back through the pages of this book and write down some of the practices that take place in the home.

The custom of kissing a mezuza shows respect and love for the word of God inside it

A reminder at the door

The child in the photograph is touching a **mezuza**. Like tefillin, a mezuza is a sacred object for Jews and it is nailed to the doorpost as a sign that the home is a Jewish home. The 'mezuza' is, strictly speaking, the parchment scroll inside the case which contains the first two paragraphs of the Shema.

The outer casing can be made of almost anything and Jewish art throughout the ages has tried to make the mezuza case as attractive as possible. It is fixed, sloping inwards, on the upper end of the right-hand doorpost of every living space in the house, so not only is there one on the front door but there is also one on each of the bedroom and living-room doors as well.

On arrival in a new home, mezuzot (the plural of mezuza) should be fixed up within six weeks. It is quite common for mezuzot to be given as a wedding gift so that the new couple can equip their new home properly. Like the child in the photograph, many Jews have the custom of touching a mezuza with their fingertips and kissing their fingertips as a sign of respect as they pass.

Moving house

When a Jewish family moves home, the mezuzot should not be left behind unless a Jewish family is known to be moving in.

Since it is a sacred object it would be wrong to leave one on the doorpost if there is no real confidence that it will be treated properly. On the other hand, if the new residents are Jews the mezuzot must not be removed because one Jew should not make it more difficult for another to fulfil a mitzva.

ASSIGNMENTS

● Read the account of the Exodus from Egypt in the Bible (Exodus 12). Some people suggest that the mezuza echoes an event in this important moment in Jewish history. What event is it? If they are right, what significance does this give the mezuza?

● Design and make in wood, clay, plastic or cardboard a mezuza case. Write out the first sentence of the Shema in Hebrew (shown below) in your finest calligraphic writing, without mistakes, to go inside. (Remember to write from right to left, and if you really want a challenge write it with a quill-pen!) When you have finished, write down an account of what it was like to do this task, what decisions you had to make and what thoughts came to mind.

שמע ישראל ה׳ אלקינו ה׳ אחד׃

'Listen Israel, the Lord is our God, the Lord is One.'

● Putting a mezuza on the front door has not always been an easy thing. In some societies anti-semitic prejudices have led to attacks on Jews. Script and act out a play in which a teenage son or daughter believes that the mezuza should be removed for the family's safety.

KEY WORDS

mitzva   mezuza

KEEPING KOSHER

The business of keeping **kosher** is such an important part of Jewish practice that it could well be one of the few facts that most people know about Jews. Nearly everyone knows that Jews do not eat pig meat, for example. However, the laws of kashrut (what is kosher and what is not) go much further than that. 'Kosher' means 'fitting' or 'correct' and it applies to all sorts of Jewish laws, not only food.

A mezuza that has the wrong text inside it is not kosher, a hanukia where the eight candle holders are not on the same level is not kosher and a ketuba (marriage contract) which is not properly signed or written is also not kosher. (See also page 33.)

Jews vary in their observance of kosher food laws. Some Jews will not even eat in a place where the utensils and plates have been used for non-kosher food. They may seek a guarantee from a rabbi, such as a seal of approval, that the food they buy is kosher.

Others are careful about the ingredients but less concerned about utensils. They may eat in an ordinary restaurant but will check if the frying was done in non-kosher fat. They will also check the ingredients listed by the manufacturer on the package when buying food.

Some will only be concerned about what they can see and will not check the ingredients. Others simply do not observe the food laws, but may just draw the line at pork or prawns.

Kosher food

The food laws of kashrut make requirements such as the separating of milk and meat foods (Exodus 23:19) and not eating unacceptable fish and seafood (Leviticus 11):

Anything in the seas or the rivers that lacks either fins or scales, whether they are water insects, fish or water mammals, is forbidden to you.

[Leviticus 11:10]

'I think you can get too fanatical about kashrut. Obviously I wouldn't eat anything that was really treif [non-kosher] but when the Bible was written they couldn't have been thinking about additives, could they?'

'I think kashrut was very important when the majority of the world had unhygienic standards and it's quite clear that it kept the Jews alive in the Middle Ages when the Black Death was ravaging the Christian community. But nowadays it's all out of date. Modern methods of food production have overtaken what was revolutionary biblical teaching 3,000 years ago.'

But for some Jews keeping kashrut has a special importance in the modern world:

'The laws of kashrut are even more necessary than ever before. It's so easy for Jews to mix in with non-Jews and lose their identity nowadays. In the past they didn't let us. So we need a way to keep our identity and remember all the time how we owe a debt to God. The more detailed your kashrut is the better, because it makes you think about every

little choice you make. Most people's religion only affects them just from time to time, but with kashrut, religion affects me pretty well every waking moment.'

ASSIGNMENTS

● Imagine that the three Jews quoted above were trying to get together for a meal. Write the conversation that might take place.

● You have some Jewish friends coming for dinner. Plan a meal that would be suitable for them if they were strict about kashrut.

KEY WORDS

kosher

A kosher takeaway in London

COUNTING YOUR BLESSINGS

If one believes in God as a creator and a guide throughout life and history then it follows that everything that exists and happens is due to God. One way that Jews have of remembering this is to make a statement or blessing about it. Usually 'blessing' means something good, for example 'the corner shop is a blessing'. We also use the word to mean approval as in 'she gave me her blessing'. In the Bible, parents sometimes 'bless' their children.

● Turn to Genesis 49 and find out what 'blessing' means when Jacob blesses his sons.

The Talmud recommends that one hundred blessings should be said each day. This is quite a tall order but it is meant to help Jews remember God's power. In a simple form it is a statement of faith.

A blessing for every occasion

To help fulfil this recommendation Jews have ready-made blessings for every situation. The first type is said when fulfilling a mitzva:

'You are blessed, Lord our God, King of the Universe, who has made us holy with your commandments and has commanded us to . . .'

On eating matza at the Seder the blessing would end '. . . and has commanded us to eat matza.' By doing this, Jews note that they are not eating matza because they are hungry but out of obedience to God's will.

The second type of blessing is simple. It acknowledges God as the force behind everything, good or bad. For example, the blessing on eating an apple is: 'You are blessed, Lord our God, King of the Universe, who creates the fruit of the tree.' However, if there is bad news it is: 'You are blessed, Lord our God, King of the Universe, who is a true judge.'

Blessings are not thanksgivings. Jews are not pleased to hear bad news but they recognise that even unfortunate events are somehow in God's system even though in practice this is sometimes very difficult to accept.

The hardest blessing

'The hardest blessing I ever found myself saying – I only said it because the rabbi said I was supposed to – was the one praising God as a "just judge" when I was told that my mother had died. Praising God for the miracle of the apple you are about to eat just puts into words what you might be thinking anyway. Praising God for diversity when you see someone with a handicap is a good positive way to look at them and the world. But this one made no sense. I'm only starting to understand it now – but it did comfort me to say it, in a strange sort of way, even though I disagreed with what I was saying as I said it – or I thought I did. . . .'

'You are blessed, Lord our God, King of the Universe, who . . .'

ASSIGNMENTS

● Look at the picture and complete the caption with as many blessings as you can find in the picture. Explain why you see each of these things as a blessing.

● Write a diary of one day in your life headed 'A Day of Blessings'. Note down everything that happens that you think is a blessing and say why. When you have finished say how this has helped you to understand the Jewish idea of a blessing.

● Reread the last quotation and write the dialogue that might have taken place between this man and the rabbi when he was told the blessing he should say.

IS GOD HOMELESS?

The Tenakh says that King Solomon built the Temple in Jerusalem as a resting place for the Ark of the Covenant and a home for the Shekhina, God's particular presence.

When this Temple was destroyed and the Jews were taken into captivity in Babylon they developed the **synagogue**, a place where they could meet together, study, pray and remember Jerusalem.

> How shall we sing the Lord's song in a
>   foreign land?
> If I forget you, O Jerusalem, let my
>   right hand wither!
> Let my tongue stick to the roof of my
>   mouth,
>   if I do not remember you.
>
> [Psalm 137]

Fifty years later their prayers were answered and they returned to Jerusalem. They rebuilt the Temple but did not do away with synagogues. For five hundred years or more Jews had both the Temple in Jerusalem and synagogues throughout the Jewish world. When the second Temple was destroyed by the Romans in 70 CE, only the synagogues remained.

> Come let us wipe them out as a nation,
> let the name of Israel be remembered no
> more.
>
> [The Midrash]

The picture shows a carving from the Titus' triumphal arch in Rome. On it is carved his victory in destroying the Temple and carrying off the furniture. It is from this that we have an idea of what the seven-branched candelabra from the Temple was like. Presumably Titus thought that by destroying the Temple he had taken the heart out of the Jewish people. However, he had overlooked the hundreds of synagogues throughout the Roman Empire and beyond.

The synagogue is not a replacement Temple. The two main features of the Temple – priests and sacrifices – do not exist in the synagogue; it performs a quite different function as more of a community centre. The closest substitute for the Temple might be the Jewish home. The parents become the priests, the table the altar, and the meals – properly prepared according to the laws of kashrut – become the sacrifices. God is by no means homeless. He has homes all over the world.

> Even the sparrow finds a home,
> and the swallow a nest for herself,
> where she may lay her young,
> at your altars, Lord of the heavens,
> my King and my God.
>
> [Psalm 84]

ASSIGNMENTS

● Imagine that you were a twentieth-century Jew looking at the carving in the picture. The arch was built to show that the Romans had conquered and enslaved the Jews. Write an essay or a poem based on your thoughts as you stand and look at this ruined monument.

● Is it important for God to be provided with a home? If so why? Debate this in class and write up your own summary of this debate. Take into account the Jewish ideas mentioned above.

KEY WORDS

synagogue

PEACE IN THE WORLD

Jews are not pacifists. They do not believe in peace at *any* cost. In the Bible God tells them that sometimes they must fight, that self-defence is justified. There are several rules to ensure that a war only starts if there is no alternative and that the damage is kept to a minimum.

The rules of war

1 You should not start hostilities. You can land the first punch or fire the first shot (you need not wait until you are shot) but you cannot strike until you are sure that the other side will not back off.
2 You must deliver a clear warning of the consequence of not backing off. They must know what might happen.
3 You must offer a chance of peace and give your conditions. They must have a way of avoiding the fight.
4 While carrying out an attack, you should not damage the environment indiscriminately. The Torah forbids the destroying of fruit trees when besieging a city.
5 One must always be prepared to discuss peace.

Peace Now

The word 'peace' in Hebrew is 'Shalom', a word also used for hello and goodbye. The psalms say that Torah leads to peace and Jews have always been taught to encourage peace.

Keep your tongue from evil,
and your lips from speaking deceit.
Depart from evil and do good,
seek peace and pursue it.

[Psalm 34]

The photograph shows Israelis demonstrating against Israel's involvement in Lebanon in 1982. Israel's population is only about three million so a demonstration with 60,000 people is very significant. When it takes place during a war it shows that feeling is running very high. Even some soldiers in the Israeli Army disagreed with their country's policy. This comment is from a 29-year-old captain in the Israeli Army who was a corporal at the time of the Lebanon conflict:

'I didn't agree with our staying in Lebanon. We should have come straight out after we'd given the Palestinian terrorists a bloody nose. Obviously we had to go in there and get them off our backs. We couldn't just sit in little Israel letting them use Lebanon as a terrorist base to attack our farms and families.

But Jews aren't made to be aggressors. We just need to defend ourselves. Sometimes we have to strike first because modern warfare moves so fast and we're too small to allow for a margin of error. The first war we lose will be the last war we fight. But still we must be defending and not being the aggressor. That's why some of us set up the group Yesh Gevul ['There's a Limit']. It's not quite a peace group. We want to serve in the army, we owe it to our country, but we also owe our country our moral sense of how far we should go.'

ASSIGNMENTS

● In 1982 Britain was also involved in fighting. Why was protest in Britain against the Falklands War tiny compared to the strength of feeling in Israel against the war in Lebanon?

● Are there any situations in which you think it is justified to fight? In groups produce your own guidelines for war. Debate your conclusions with other groups in the class. Think about how you would apply the 'rules of war' in a nuclear war or when chemical weapons were a threat.

● Carefully reread the comment by the Israeli. Imagine you were one of his soldiers. How far would you agree or disagree with him? Write your response to his statement.

'Nation shall not lift up sword against nation'
[Isaiah 2:4]

THE VALUE OF LIFE

Jews believe that all human lives are of equal value and that people must firstly look after their own lives and secondly try to preserve the lives of others. According to Judaism, a swimmer who leaves someone to drown is responsible for their death. Furthermore, if you decided to shoot someone to make certain death less painful, you would be guilty of murder, by shortening their life if only by a moment.

If a besieger says, 'Give me ten people, or I will wipe out everyone', the rulers must say, 'So be it'. If they selected ten people, they would be guilty of their murder. If, however, the besieger says, 'Give me these named people, or I will wipe out everyone', the rulers must hand those named people over. If the city were wiped out, the named people would also die. Handing them over saves all the unnamed people. The rulers would be guilty of the murder of the unnamed people if they protected the named people.

[Talmud]

This situation became relevant during the Nazi Holocaust. Many times the Nazis asked Jewish community leaders to identify people for the 'work camps' which many rightly suspected were death camps. Whatever they did, it seems that someone suffered. If the Jewish leaders refused to co-operate, there were often huge reprisals. If they did co-operate, they helped the Nazis and destroyed the self-respect that helped them to survive.

The doctor's dilemma

Doctors often have to make professional decisions on saving life. Jews believe that this should be a medical decision and not a judgement on who is worth saving. No one can decide whose life is worth keeping and whose is not. The doctor must not play God.

Euthanasia, killing people because we think they may be suffering or serving no further purpose, would be murder, according to Jewish tradition. If a foetus were a human being then abortion would also be regarded as murder. However, Jews believe that a foetus becomes human, that is receives its soul, when it is born. If a foetus is threatening the health of the mother then one should abort it in order to try and save the mother. A not-yet human life is not as important as a human life. This would be seen as killing but not murder.

ASSIGNMENTS

- Imagine you are a Jew. Look at the photo then write a letter to a non-Jewish friend explaining why you are unable to march under the banner in the demonstration even though you may feel that abortion on demand is wrong.

- In small groups, imagine you are a Jewish community council under Nazi control. The community has ten children, twenty teenagers, thirty young adults, twenty people aged 40–60, ten aged 60–70, and ten aged 70–80. Among them are five with mental and five with physical handicaps. The Nazis tell you to choose the next ten people to go to the camps. If you don't, they will. Write down your response to this demand as a declaration of your community's rights and beliefs. Include the decision you have come to, giving your reasons.

WHAT WILL PEOPLE THINK?

● Can you think of any situation in which you have felt you should behave in a certain way because of what people might think about you, your group or your family?

Very often the thing that controls our behaviour is concern about what other people might think of us. Jews are often conscious that when they do something bad, other people might not only disapprove of them but they might also make general criticisms about all Jews because of what they have done.

Hillul Hashem

Deeply rooted in the way Jews think about themselves is the idea that not only will people judge other Jews in the light of Jewish behaviour, but they will also judge God and his teaching. As a result, when a Jew does something wrong publicly this is often called a **Hillul Hashem**. This means a 'cursing of God'. Put simply, by misbehaving, the Jew has probably led other people to think less well of the God Jews are guided by. So someone might say that a Jew who has committed a crime has also committed a 'Hillul Hashem'.

Kiddush Hashem

A good deed, however, can act as a **Kiddush Hashem** ('making God holy'),

by helping people appreciate God more. This sets a very demanding task. It is not just about what the neighbours might say about us, or even about our friends and family. It also implies that Jews must try to improve moral standards in the world. Isaiah the Prophet said that Jews should be 'a light to the nations'. While Jews do not send out missionaries, or try to convert people, this idea of 'Kiddush Hashem' shows that Jews do have a sense of mission to the world. Here is an everyday example of it:

'When I went back to the bus conductor to pay my fare before I got off, I knew no one would have minded if I hadn't paid. Other people were getting off without paying. But I was wearing my kipa [skull cap] and I wanted the conductor and the passengers to think "What decent, honest people Jews are!" People tend to generalise from what they see, so I suppose I was trying to do a small Kiddush Hashem.'

ASSIGNMENTS

● Can you think of a recent situation in which you have done something because of what other people might think? Think of another situation in which you have *not* done something because of what other people might think. Write an essay or story about one or other of these situations explaining why you behaved in the way you did.

● Attacks on Jews and Jewish sites still happen all over the world. Sometimes they are verbal attacks or vicious articles in newspapers; sometimes they are physical, and occasionally they are fatal. Look at the photograph. Imagine you are a community of Jews in this locality. Remembering Hillul Hashem and Kiddush Hashem decide how you should react to this event. Write a leaflet to distribute among local Jews advising them about this problem and how to react to it.

KEY WORDS

Hillul Hashem   Kiddush Hashem

TZEDAKA

The word **tzedaka** means 'righteousness', and the idea of tzedaka means that rich and poor must help those who cannot provide for themselves. A rich person can of course give more but a poor person must give something.

British Jews obviously pay taxes like everyone else and so support the national welfare system but, in addition, the Jewish community voluntarily taxes itself to provide schools, hospitals, old age homes, sheltered housing, education, child care, counsel for the bereaved, marriage guidance, the deaf association, the blind society, day care for the elderly, kosher meals on wheels and social provision for

those with mental and physical disabilities.

PHAB (Physically Handicapped and Able Bodied) was one of the first organisations in Britain for people with physical disabilities to do activities together with able-bodied people. The children in the photograph are at Ravenswood Village, a world leader in the provision for those with mental disabilities.

The Torah in action

The Torah insists that the rich have a responsibility to the poor. Supporting the poor is not just a virtue but a requirement.

> You shall not oppress a hired servant who is poor and needy, whether he is an Israelite or one of the immigrants who are in your land within your towns; you shall give him his wage on the day he earns it, before the sun goes down (for he is poor, and needs it).
>
> Deuteronomy 24:14]

This makes the teaching about tzedaka very important, but to understand it you have to do it, as this American headteacher explains:

> 'You can't teach about tzedaka without doing some, so we require of all our kids that they set up a project of some sort. Some visit an elderly person or someone housebound, some set up some fundraising activity, some spend time at a local school for the blind, while others give up a night a week to man our soup run for the down-and-outs in the centre of town. You can't ask too much of them because they're all under Bar or Batmitzvah but if you start them young they'll learn that you get more out of tzedaka than you give and it will become a lifelong habit. Some of our best pupils have donated a large proportion of their Bat/Barmitzvah presents to whatever their pet cause is. Obviously giving money is easier than giving time, but many of our children graduate from one to the other as they get older and realise what they can do.'

ASSIGNMENTS

- Imagine you are one of the women helping the children in the picture. Someone asks you why you do this work and what satisfaction you receive from it. Write a reply explaining the Jewish point of view but include your own feelings about doing this kind of work.

- You are asked to give a short talk on the welfare work that is carried out by Jewish people. Research this further, reading about organisations such as PHAB and ORT (Organisation for Rehabilitation through Training), and then plan and prepare your talk.

KEY WORDS

tzedaka

EDUCATION

You shall teach these words [the Torah] carefully to your children, repeating them when you sit at home, when you walk in the street, when you go to bed and when you get up.

[Deuteronomy 6:7]

Another important value in the Jewish community is education. This is not surprising bearing in mind that all of Judaism is based on the study and understanding of a book. Traditionally the highest status was given to a rabbi or scholar. After leaving school some Jews take a year off to study in a Jewish college.

Most Jewish children learn Hebrew and Torah at a school (usually known as hayder) attached to their synagogue. This often involves attendance on Sundays and at mid-week classes after ordinary school.

'We don't have enough time in hayder to teach all we want. There's the Hebrew language, there's Bible and 3,000 years' worth of literature, there's a very long history, hundreds of traditions, laws and customs, songs, prayers and stories, the geography of Israel, practices for a dozen festivals, food laws and so on. Not only that, we try to teach it all to the poor bairns when they're tired after a hard day at school or when their non-Jewish friends are out playing. It's still not easy to be a Jew!'

In some towns there are also Jewish schools. One of the first free schools in Britain was the Jews' Free School, established in the nineteenth century. It was destroyed in the Second World War blitz.

'I don't think my parents ever felt the need to send me to a Jewish school. I went to hayder every Sunday morning, and after school on Mondays and Wednesdays, from when I was six to just after my Barmitzvah. They wanted me to carry on after that but I felt my exams were more important. Probably a Jewish school would have solved that.'

What is Jewish education for?

Here are two Jewish points of view:

'If a parent doesn't take every opportunity to instil a love and enjoyment of Judaism into their child, then they only have themselves to blame if their children marry out. Every Jewish parent wants Jewish grandchildren. Well, it's not going to happen by leaving the middle link ignorant.'

'I'm pleased I had a good Jewish education at a Jewish school. Because of it, I know how to deal with anti-semitism and anti-semitic comments at college. I can be proud of being a Jew whatever they say, instead of just being confused as some of my friends are.'

ASSIGNMENTS

● Imagine you are a Jewish child, aged 11, considering which school you would like to go to. Write the discussion you might have with your parents about the possibility of going to a Jewish school where you could study everything under one roof.

● Why do Jews value education so highly? Record a dialogue between a Jewish parent and their child. Imagine that the parent runs a small business and the child is trying to decide whether to study chemistry at university or go straight into the family business. (Think carefully about the parent's experiences, how they came to be in Britain, and why they are involved in business rather than something associated with study.)

Glossary

Aggada Jewish teachings through story

Atonement An attempt to correct past errors

Barmitzvah Coming of age for boys at 13

Batmitzvah Coming of age for girls at 12

bima Central platform in a synagogue where the Torah is read

Brit Mila Circumcision as a sign of God's relationship with the Jews

circumcision Cutting away the foreskin

Exodus Escape of the Israelites from Egyptian slavery

Hanuka Winter festival of lights commemorating the recapture and rededication of the Temple

hanukia Candelabra on which the Hanuka lights are lit

Hillul Hashem Behaviour that is likely to lead people to think badly of Jews and of the God they follow

Kaddish Mourner's prayer which praises God

Ketuvim The least authoritative part of the Tenakh, including the poetry of the Psalms and the stories of Esther and Ruth

Kiddush Hashem Behaviour that is likely to lead people to think well of Jews and of the God they follow

kosher Acceptable according to the rules of the Torah

Maccabees Family who successfully won back the Temple at the time of the first Hanuka

matza Unleavened bread used at Pesakh

Messiah The ideal ruler who will create a Golden Age

Messianic Age The Golden Age that Jews hope and work for

mezuza (plural: mezuzot) Parchment scroll with first two paragraphs of the Shema, fixed in a case to the doorpost

Mishna Written summary of the Oral Torah

mitzva (plural: mitzvot) Rule or good deed according to the Torah

mohel Circumciser

Nevi'im General name for the Prophetic books of the Bible

Orthodox Those who follow the teachings of the Oral Torah closely

Pesakh Spring New Year festival commemorating the Exodus from Egypt

Progressive Those who do not believe the Torah and its traditions are binding

Rosh Hashana Autumn New Year festival starting the cycle of repentance

Seder Pesakh eve service telling the Exodus story

Shabbat Day of rest, recreation and spirituality

Shekhina The 'presence' of God

shel rosh Head piece of tefillin

shel yad Hand and arm piece of tefillin

Shema The most important Jewish prayer stating, among other things, belief in one God

Shiva First week of intensive mourning

shofar Animal (usually ram's) horn blown on Rosh Hashana

Siddur The Jewish prayer book

Simkhat Torah Festival which celebrates the ending and recommencement of the annual cycle of reading the Torah

sofer Scribe

synagogue Community meeting place

Talmud Fundamental encyclopaedia of Jewish law and discussion consisting of the Mishna and Gemara

tefillin Prayer aids worn on head and arm during weekday morning services

Temple The central Jewish building until it was destroyed by the Romans

Tenakh Hebrew (Jewish) Bible

teshuva Repentance

Torah All of Jewish teaching; particularly the first five books of the Bible

tzedaka Justice and charity

Yom Kippur Holiest day of the Jewish year, the climax Day of Atonement

Zionism Belief that Jews have a right to a State of their own in Israel

Index

Further reading

The Authorised Daily Prayer Book, with introductory notes from the Chief Rabbi Lord Immanuel Jakobovits. Eyre & Spottiswood, 1990 (*Siddur, use of Ketuvim, life cycle rituals and blessings*)

Hertz, Chief Rabbi J.H. (ed.) *The Pentateuch and Haftorahs*, Soncino, London 1962 (*Torah with commentary, weekly reading from Nevi'im*)

Raphael, C. *A Feast of History*, Weidenfeld & Nicolson, 1972 (*Seder service with explanatory notes*)

Gilbert, M. *Jewish History Atlas*, Weidenfeld & Nicolson, 3rd r.e. 1985

The Jewish Chronicle (*a weekly newspaper*)

Lawton, C.A. *Israel* in *Passport* series, Franklin Watts, 1989

— *The Seder Handbook: A Guide and Text for the Passover Meal*, Central Jewish Lecture & Information Committee, 1984 (*available from CJLIC, Board of Deputies of British Jews, Woburn House, Upper Woburn Place, London WC1H 0EP; the CJLIC provides teaching material on Jews and Judaism for schools, including filmstrips*)

Rose, J. *Jewish Worship* in *World Religions* series, Cassell, n.e. 1988

Steinsaltz, A. *The Essential Talmud*, Basic Books/Harper Colophon, New York 1976

Wood, A. *Judaism*, Batsford, 1984

Acknowledgements

We are grateful to the following for permission to reproduce photographs:

Ancient Art & Architecture Collection, pages 21, 50; Barnaby's Picture Library, page 8; Colorific, page 57 (photo: Brian Harris); Barbara Gingold, Jerusalem, page 32; Sonia Halliday Photographs, pages 31 (photo: Jane Taylor), 43; Hutchison Library, pages 40 (photo: Liba Taylor), 47 (photo: Adrian Evans), 60 (photo: Liba Taylor); Institute of Contemporary History & Wiener Library Ltd, page 7; Collection Israel Museum, Jerusalem, page 13 (photo: Israel Museum/David Harris); R M Kneller, page 36; Clive Lawton, page 49; Magnum, page 4 (photo: Cornell Capa); Panos Pictures, page 10 (photo: Ron Gilling); Picturepoint, page 25; Zev Radovan, Jerusalem, pages 16, 26, 29; Ravenswood Foundation, Jewish Society for Mentally Handicapped, London, page 58; Select Photo Agency & Picture Library, page 15 (photo: David Hoffman); Barry Sheridan, Jerusalem, page 53; Juliette Soester, pages 22, 35; Frank Spooner Pictures/Gama, page 54; © Israel Talby, 1989, Jerusalem, Israel, pages 38, 44; Collection Tel Aviv Museum of Art. Gift of Sidney J Lamon, New York, 1939, page 18.

Picture research assisted by Andrea Stern

Cover: Celebrating a Bar Mitzvah at the Western Wall, Jerusalem, Israel. (photo: Picturepoint)

The painting on page 49 is by Juliette Harris.

LONGMAN GROUP UK LIMITED
*Longman House, Burnt Mill, Harlow,
Essex CM2O 2JE, England
and Associated Companies throughout the world.*

First published 1992
ISBN   0 582 02969 4

*Set in 11/14 Garamond
Produced by Longman Group (FE) Ltd
Printed in Hong Kong*